W9-AVA-066

The Boston Tea Party
No Taxation Without Representation

Alicia Tovar

PowerKiDS press™

NEW YORK

Published in 2016 by The Rosen Publishing Group, Inc.
29 East 21st Street, New York, NY 10010

Photo Credits: Cover GraphicaArtis/Archive Photos/Getty Images; p. 5 Library of Congress Prints and Photographs
Division; p. 6 Hulton Archive/Getty Images; p. 7 Gilder Lehrman Collection, New York, USA/Bridgeman Images;
pp. 8, 20 © North Wind Picture Archives; p. 9 Photo Researchers/Science Source/Getty Images; p. 11 Gilder
Lehrman Collection, New York, USA/Bridgeman Images; p. 12 DEA Picture Library/Getty Images; pp. 13, 15 MPI/
Archive Photos/Getty Images; pp. 16, 17, 19 Private Collection/Peter Newark American Pictures/Bridgeman
Images; p. 21 © Collection of the New-York Historical Society, USA/Bridgeman Images

Library of Congress Cataloging-in-Publication Data

Tovar, Alicia.
The Boston Tea Party : no taxation without representation / Alicia Tovar. -- First edition.
    pages cm. -- (Spotlight on American history)
 Includes bibliographical references and index.
 ISBN 978-1-4994-1726-5 (library bound) -- ISBN 978-1-4994-1742-5 (pbk.) -- ISBN 978-1-4994-1724-1
(6-pack)
1. Boston Tea Party, Boston, Mass., 1773--Juvenile literature. I. Title.
 E215.7.T68 2016
 973.3'115--dc23
                                    2015014122

Manufactured in the United States of America

CPSIA Compliance Information: Batch #WS15PK: For Further Information contact Rosen Publishing, New York, New York at 1-800-237-9932

CONTENTS

PAYING FOR ENGLAND'S WAR

English men and women came to America to live in **colonies** in the 1600s and 1700s. These **colonists** were **citizens** of Britain. They did not, however, have any say in the laws that the British government made. Not having a say in the laws made their lives harder.

The French also had colonies in North America. Their colonies were located in what is now Canada and the middle part of the United States, from what is now Michigan south to Louisiana. The French wanted more land, so in 1754 the French attacked farms in the British colonial areas. This started the French and Indian War. The English colonists went to war against the French and won.

George III was the king of Great Britain at this time. The king was glad the colonists had won the war, but the fighting had cost his country a lot of money. The king and his prime minister decided to tax the colonists to raise money.

In 1764, the British made a law to tax the trade on sugar. In 1765, another law, the Stamp Act, put a tax on printed material. The American colonists thought this was unfair. They believed that they should be free from "taxation without representation."

THE STAMP ACT DENOUNCED.

In 1765, colonists organized to protest the British Stamp Act. The act put a tax on printed materials such as newspapers. The colonists argued that the tax was illegal. They tried to force the stamp tax collectors to quit.

TEA SMUGGLING

In 1767, the British passed a new tax on tea and other household goods such as paper and glass. These new taxes were called the Townshend Acts. American colonists would now have to pay three cents extra for each pound (454 grams) of English tea they bought.

An American colonist reads a royal notice of a tax on tea in the colonies as a British soldier stands nearby. The tax on tea was a part of the Townshend Acts. In 1770, Parliament repealed most of the Townshend taxes, but the tax on tea stayed in place.

This drawing shows British troops coming into Boston. The troops were sent to make sure that colonists paid the taxes forced on them by the Townshend Acts.

Most American colonists were not very upset because they did not drink British tea. They drank Dutch tea **smuggled** into American **ports**. Drinking Dutch tea was an act of resistance against the British government.

In 1768, Englishmen who worked for the **customs** office in Massachusetts asked the English navy for help. They wanted the navy to stop the tea smugglers from coming into Boston. The English sent a warship with 50 cannons to Boston Harbor. The smugglers paid no attention to the warship. Tension between Britain and the American colonists was growing.

THE BOSTON MASSACRE

The American colonists did not want to pay British taxes on things such as paper, paint, and tea. They spoke out against the taxes, but the British kept taxing them. They also sent more soldiers to American cities. The soldiers were there to make sure the tax laws were followed.

This woodcut shows colonial boys in Boston teasing a British soldier. Colonists called British soldiers lobsterbacks because they wore red coats.

The growing number of British soldiers in Boston angered the colonists. They felt that their rights as free citizens were being threatened. The anger of the colonists turned into violence at the Boston Massacre.

On March 5, 1770, a fight broke out in Boston between angry American colonists and British soldiers. The British soldiers fired their guns at unarmed Americans. Five men died. This event was called the Boston **Massacre**.

The British became worried about the violence in the colonies. In 1770, Parliament repealed the Townshend Acts. The only tax that continued was on tea. Some colonists started to drink British tea again, but some still refused. Many American colonists, however, did not like Parliament's control over them. They also did not like British soldiers in their cities.

THE TEA ACT OF 1773

Most tea in America was brought in illegally after 1770. The American colonists were no longer buying British tea. A trading company called the British East India Company was losing a lot of money because the American colonists would not buy British tea. In 1772, the company had 18 million pounds (8.16 million kilograms) of unsold tea.

In 1773, British Parliament passed the Tea Act to save the company. This law made sure that tea could be bought only from merchants chosen by the East India Company. The company could sell tea at a price that was less than the price of tea smuggled into America, but there was still a tax.

The British thought the American colonists would be happy to drink tea that was cheap and legal. Instead, the Americans were angry. They thought the Tea Act was a sneaky way of making them pay the tea tax. They felt they were being pressured to give in to Parliament. Parliament wanted to force taxation without representation on the colonists.

TO THE

Commiſſioners

APPOINTED by the *EAST-INDIA* COMPANY, for the SALE of

TEA, in America.

GENTLEMEN,

YOUR Appointment, which is notoriouſly deſigned to enforce the Act of 7th G. III. *for raiſing a Revenue in America*, juſtly claims the Attention of every Man, who wiſhes well to this Country : And you need not be ſurprized to find the Eyes of ALL now fixed on you ; as on Men, who have it in their Power to ward off the moſt dangerous Stroke, that has been ever meditated againſt the Liberties of America.

You have before you the Examples of many of your unhappy Countrymen, I mean *ſome* of the STAMP MASTERS ; Examples, which, if properly attended to, may convince you, how fooliſh, how dangerous it is, to undertake to force the loathſome Pills of Slavery and Oppreſſion down the Throats of a free, independent and determined People.—— Your *Appointment* is exactly ſimilar to that of our late STAMP MASTERS—They were commiſſioned to enforce one Revenue Act ; you to execute another—The Stamp and Tea Laws were both deſigned to raiſe a Revenue, and to eſtabliſh *Parliamentary Deſpotiſm* in America.

There cannot therefore be any Difference in your Appointments ; except in this ; that their Office as *Stamp Men* ſavoured ſtrongly of the Nature of *Exciſe Officers* ; whilſt you, in the Execution of your *Duty*, may retain ſome feint Reſemblance of the decent Characters of *Factors*. But let not Names deceive you :—Your Characters as Stamp Maſters and Tea Commiſſioners have a ſtrong and near Affinity. They and you could boaſt, that you were our Brethren ; they and you owe at leaſt SUPPORT, if not LIFE, to America ; and what characterizes the two Employments in the ſtrongeſt Manner, they and you were marked out, by the Conſpirators againſt our Rights, to give the laſt, the finiſhing Stroke to Freedom in this Country.——Stange indeed ! that Americans ſhould be pitched on to violate the Privileges of Americans !

You cannot believe, that the *Tea Act*, with Reſpect to its Deſign and Tendency, differs in one ſingle Point from the *Stamp Act*.—If there be any Difference the *Tea Act* is the more dang[...]
of Peopl[...]
Act, mor[...]
diſcover [...]
fer his P[...]
without [...]
therefore[...]
under th[...]
afterward[...]
the Price[...]
imported[...]
Man does[...]
It is in vain then to ſeek for any Diſtinction between the two Employments.—To Americans it muſt be a Matter of Indifference, by what Stile or Title you may think proper to demean yourſelves ; whether STAMP MASTERS or TEA

try—What Appointments at Home or Abroad can ever make up to you the Loſs of your Brethren's Affections ? What Appointments can atone to your Children, for the cruel, moſt horrid, Predicament to which you may ſubject them ?—You have given them a Birth-Right in America ; which you found a Land of Liberty and ſocial Enjoyment—Let them therefore peaceably and happily inherit it.—You can have no Proſpect of ſubjugating America, that you or they may become ſovereign Princes ; if you have, your Proſpect indeed muſt be extenſive ; and in my Opinion, productive of every Miſchief to them and you : Beſides, if you mean to eſtabliſh your Children happily, they will derive more real Satisfaction as PRIMI INTER PARES ; to which their Virtue may entitle them in a free Country ; than they can ever enjoy as TYRANTS over a Band of Slaves.—But ſuch I truſt cannot be your Motives.—You have already filled ſome of the moſt important Offices in the American State ;—you have hitherto acted on the broad and ſafe Baſis of diſintereſted Virtue ; by diſcharging many public Duties without Fee or Reward : And you cannot now act ſo directly repugnant to your former virtuous Actions ; ſo contrary to the Sentiments of your watchful Countrymen, as to be induced by *the paltry Bribe of a petty Commiſſion*, to rivet the Shackles of Slavery on your American Brethren.

If the Eaſt India Company can eſtabliſh Warehouſes in America for the Sale of TEA *on which a Duty is impoſed for the Purpoſe of raiſing a Revenue in America*, they may vend, in like Manner, any other Articles of their Trade. On ſuch other Articles, Parliament may impoſe a Duty to be paid in America ; and the Company's Commiſſioners will no doubt take ſpecial Care to pay ſuch Duty : and *reimburſe their Conſtituents, by fleecing it from the People.*—Thus the Impoſition may be encreaſed at Pleaſure ; and America be ſubjugated without the Poſſibility of Redemption.

It has been alledged *by ſome* that your Friends in England, to whoſe ſpecial Grace and Favor you are entitled for the important Commiſſion, *have given Security, in very high Sums*[...]

This letter protests the tea tax as a way to raise money for Britain. The colonists felt it was unfair to be forced to pay taxes since they had no one to represent them in the British government. This was called taxation without representation.

Execution of any whimſical Schemes the Miniſtry of the [...] India Company might chalk out for you : All the Security given amounts to no more than this, that, if you ſhould *undertake and be permitted to enforce the REVENUE ACT in Ameri*-

SPEAKING OUT AGAINST THE TEA ACT

Samuel Adams was an American **patriot**. He thought that by paying taxes, the American colonists were allowing the British to tell them what to do. Adams taught Americans that their opinions were important. He told them that they could take action to change unfair laws.

After the British passed the Tea Act in September of 1773, Adams found out that three tea ships were

Samuel Adams organized Boston's Sons of Liberty. The Sons of Liberty were responsible for the Boston Tea Party. After the revolution, Adams worked for the government of Massachusetts. Adams became the governor of Massachusetts in 1793.

Thomas Hutchinson served as the governor of Massachusetts from 1771 to 1774. He was replaced in 1774 because he was unable to control the colonists.

heading for Boston. If the Americans paid the tax on the British tea that the ships were carrying, they would be saying that the British had a right to tax them. Adams wrote a letter saying that the Tea Act was unfair. He sent the letter to Thomas Hutchinson, the governor of Massachusetts. The governor was **loyal** to King George III. He paid no attention to Samuel Adams.

SAMUEL ADAMS'S STRATEGY

Samuel Adams had a plan for ending the British tea trade in Boston. He wanted to make the British tea **agents** working in Boston quit their jobs. In other ports along the Atlantic Ocean, American colonists had forced the agents to quit. Tea shipments were returned to England or stored away.

Adams wanted the tea agents in Boston to quit in front of a crowd. If the American colonists could force the tea agents to quit in public, it would show the British that the Americans had power over them.

Adams put up posters telling people to come watch the agents quit. The agents never came. The crowd was angry that the tea agents did not show up. Adams spent the next few weeks making speeches against the British government. Many American colonists agreed with what Adams said.

We the Ladys
of Edenton do
hereby Solemnly
Engage not to Conform
to that Pernicious Custom
of Drinking Tea, or that we the
aforesaid Ladys will not promote ye wear
of any Manufactore from England
untill such time that all Acts
which tend to Enslave this our
Native Country shall be Repealed

This picture shows a meeting of colonial American women. They have come together to sign an agreement promising not to drink British tea.

AMERICAN PROTESTERS TAKE ACTION

The tea ship *Dartmouth* docked in Boston Harbor in November 1773. American colonial protesters kept the tea from being unloaded. King George III decided that British customs officials could take the tea off the ship by force. Samuel Adams knew that the tea would end up in American stores. Americans would buy the tea and pay the tax on it.

This picture shows the tea ship Dartmouth *in Boston Harbor. The* Dartmouth *was one of the ships that was boarded by colonists during the Boston Tea Party.*

> **BOSTON,** December 2, 1773.
>
> WHEREAS it has been reported that a Permit will be given by the Custom-House for Landing the Tea now on Board a Vessel laying in this Harbour, commanded by Capt. HALL : THIS is to Remind the Publick, That it was solemnly voted by the Body of the People of this and the neighbouring Towns assembled at the Old-South Meeting-House on Tuesday the 30th Day of *November*, that the said Tea never should be landed in this Province, or pay one Farthing of Duty : And as the aiding or assisting in procuring or granting any such Permit for landing the said Tea or any other Tea so circumstanced, or in offering any Permit when obtained to the Master or Commander of the said Ship, or any other Ship in the same Situation, must betray an inhuman Thirst for Blood, and will also in a great Measure accelerate Confusion and Civil War : This is to assure such public Enemies of this Country, that they will be considered and treated as Wretches unworthy to live, and will be made the first Victims of our just Resentment.
>
> *The* PEOPLE.

This sign was put up in Boston on December 2, 1773. It warns citizens not to allow British tea to be unloaded in Boston Harbor.

Samuel Adams wanted to send the tea back to England. Other cities in America had sent back English tea or stored it away. In South Carolina, the tea was stored away until 1776.

On December 16, 1773, Samuel Adams and 5,000 colonists asked the governor of Massachusetts to send back the tea. The governor took his orders from King George III. He would not send the tea back.

DUMPING TEA

On December 16, 1773, Samuel Adams held a meeting at the Old South Meeting House. He met with a group of patriots called the Sons of Liberty. They planned to sneak onto the tea ships and dump the British tea into the water. Adams and his men dressed up as Native Americans so they would not be recognized. Before they left to go to where the ships were docked, they shouted "Boston Harbor a tea-pot tonight."

Samuel Adams and the Sons of Liberty snuck onto the tea ships shortly after 6 o'clock in the evening. The ships were docked in Boston Harbor. When the men got on the ships, they locked the crews of the ships below deck. They smashed open 342 chests of tea. Each chest weighed 260 pounds (118 kg). They dumped the tea into Boston Harbor.

When all the chests were empty, they swept the decks of the ships. They even shook out their shoes to make sure no tea came onto the shore. The next morning, Adams sent men to **crush** any tea that had floated onto the beach. This event was later called the Boston Tea Party.

This picture shows American colonists dressed as Native Americans dumping British tea into Boston Harbor. For many years, this event was known simply as "the destruction of the tea." It wasn't until 1826 that the event was given the name the "Boston Tea Party."

THE BRITISH KING CLOSES BOSTON HARBOR

When King George III heard about the tea being dumped, he was very angry. He wanted the American colonists to pay for the tea they had destroyed. He closed Boston Harbor and would not open it until the Americans paid for the tea.

The king sent 4,000 British soldiers to the harbor. He told the soldiers to stop ships from bringing supplies to Boston. He planned to **starve** the Bostonians until they obeyed him.

This picture shows British troops entering Boston after the Boston Tea Party. The British force was meant to keep goods from entering Boston Harbor.

Parliament passed the Boston Port Act in 1774. This act called for the port to stay closed until the people of Boston paid for the tea dumped into the harbor. This satirical drawing shows colonists helping to get food to the people of Boston.

The British wanted to punish the colonists in Massachusetts. They also wanted to prove that England still ruled the American colonies. Americans in other colonies thought King George III was being too hard on the people of Boston. They sent food and other supplies by land to Boston so the colonists would not go hungry.

THE EFFECT OF THE BOSTON TEA PARTY

Other "tea parties" were held in American cities after the Boston Tea Party. The tea parties showed that many Americans did not want to be ruled by England. American colonists wanted the British king to know that the American colonies were **united**.

Many Americans respected patriots like Samuel Adams. They wanted to help the people of Boston when England closed Boston Harbor. They wanted to show the king that they deserved the same rights as other citizens in Britain.

More and more colonists began to help each other and speak out against England. The 13 colonies were taking steps toward independence. In time they would become a single, **unified** nation called the United States of America.

GLOSSARY

agents (AY-jents) People that act for another person or group.

citizens (SIH-tih-zenz) People who are born in or who have the legal right to live in a certain country.

colonies (KAH-luh-neez) Areas in new countries where large groups of people move who are still ruled by the leaders and laws of their old country.

colonists (KAH-luh-nists) People who live in colonies.

crush (KRUSH) To destroy something by squeezing it hard.

customs (KUS-tumz) Taxes paid to a government on things brought in from a foreign country.

loyal (LOY-ul) Faithful to a person or idea.

massacre (MA-suh-ker) The killing of a group of helpless or unarmed people.

patriot (PAY-tree-ut) One who supported the independence of the American colonies.

ports (PORTS) Cities or towns where ships come to dock and trade.

smuggled (SMUH-guld) Sneaked into the country illegally.

starve (STARV) To cause people to suffer or die from hunger.

unified (YOO-nih-fyd) Joined together.

united (yoo-NY-ted) Coming together to act as a single group.

INDEX

PRIMARY SOURCE LIST

Page 5: *The Stamp Act Denounced*, artist unknown, was published in 1913 in *Lossing's History of the United States of America, Volume 3* (by Benson John Lossing). It is at the Library of Congress Prints and Photographs Division, Washington, D.C.

Page 7: *A View of the Town of Boston in New England and British Ships of War Landing Their Troops 1768* was created in May of 1770. It was engraved by Paul Revere and colored by Christian Remick. It is stored at the Gilder Lehrman Collection, New York.

Page 8: Engraving from *The Youths' History of the United States from the Discovery of America by the Northmen, to the Present Time* by Edward S. Ellis. It was published in 1893 by Cassell Publishing Company, New York. Copyrighted by O.M. Dunham, 1887.

Page 11: *To the Commissioners Appointed by the East India Company, for the Sale of Tea, in America, signed Scaevola, 1773*. This document is stored at the Gilder Lehrman Collection, New York. Scaevola was a made-up name, or pseudonym.

Page 12: *Portrait of Samuel Adams, American Statesman and Political Philosopher*, was painted by John Singleton Copley (1738 – 1815).

Page 17: This lithograph was a public warning, created by colonists on December 2, 1773. It warned colonists against accepting British tea from ships or paying any amount for it.

Page 20: Antique steel engraving from *History of the United States from the Earliest Period; with additions by Samuel L. Knapp and John Overton Chules; A New Edition, Brought Down to the Present Time, in which Are Added Biographies of the Signers of the Declaration of Independence, by W. A. Crafts; Elegantly Illustrated*. Published by Walker and Virtue, Boston, 1861, authored by John Howard Hinton.

WEBSITES

Due to the changing nature of Internet links, PowerKids Press has developed an online list of websites related to the subject of this book. This site is updated regularly. Please use this link to access the list: www.powerkidslinks.com/soah/btp